Thomas Jefferson Murrey

Cookery with a Chafing Dish

Thomas Jefferson Murrey

Cookery with a Chafing Dish

ISBN/EAN: 9783744789257

Printed in Europe, USA, Canada, Australia, Japan

Cover: Foto ©Lupo / pixelio.de

More available books at **www.hansebooks.com**

COOKERY

WITH A CHAFING DISH

BY

THOMAS J. MURREY

FORMERLY PROFESSIONAL CATERER OF THE CONTINENTAL HOTEL,
PHILADELPHIA ; ASTOR HOUSE, NEW YORK, AND
OTHER LEADING HOTELS

Author of "Salads and Sauces," "Valuable Cooking
Receipts," Etc.

NEW YORK
FREDERICK A. STOKES COMPANY
MDCCCXCI

TO

MY FRIEND

EDWARD P. BARKER

THIS UNPRETENTIOUS BUT USEFUL LITTLE WORK IS

MOST RESPECTFULLY DEDICATED

BY THE

AUTHOR.

CONTENTS.

CONTENTS.

PAGE

INTRODUCTORY.

CHAFING dish cookery is the latest fad among the amateur and professional gourmets of Gotham.

Chafing dish clubs have not only been formed in the family circle but many of the leading clubs of New York have taken up the subject with the cheerful prospect that in a few years from now, to be an Amercian will be synonymous with possessing a knowledge of the art of cookery although it has been the reverse in the past.

The sound common sense displayed in this fad shows that society is not the vapid thing our humorous journals would have us believe it to be. Society to-day is advancing so rapidly towards the practical, that not to know a great deal about cookery and dainty dining is to announce one's educational deficiencies and lack of social standing.

As chafing dish cookery is practised at table, it is not only a gustatory treat, but an intellectual entertainment as well. The palate-ravishing aromas which arise, keenly sharpen the most jaded appetite, and the preparation of the viands loosens the tongue of the most bashful, ending in useful and instructive discussion.

THE AUTHOR.

THE CHAFING DISH.

Oysters.—Put into a chafing dish a heaping table-spoonful of table butter, sprinkle over it a pinch of flour; when the butter begins to melt stir it rapidly with a wooden spoon, season with a saltspoonful of salt and a dash of cayenne, add a gill of oyster liquor, stir and simmer a few seconds then add eighteen oysters. When the gills begin to curl up they will be cooked enough; serve plain or on toast.

Oysters No. 2.—Put into a chafing dish a tea-spoonful of butter; let it become quite hot. Drain and dry in a napkin ten oysters, dredge them in a little flour, shake off the loose flour, then cook them in the butter until they are a delicate brown on both sides: season with salt and pepper.

Deviled Oysters.—Mix together a tea-spoonful of curry powder, a saltspoonful of dry mustard, a saltspoonful each of salt and white pepper and the yolk of one raw egg;

work to a paste with a table-spoonful of oil, spread this over six large or twelve small oysters. Put into a chafing dish two table-spoonfuls of olive oil; when hot add the oysters and cook well done.

Oyster Broth.—Chop up two dozen medium sized oysters, put it into a chafing dish with three half pints of oyster liquor or water, season with salt, pepper, and a walnut of butter; serve in small cups.

Quick Vegetable Soup.—Put into a chafing dish three pints of water, when it boils add two table-spoonfuls of canned macedoine, a table-spoonful of maggi bouillon, salt and pepper to taste and serve. Dried julienne which comes in paper packages may be used instead of the macedoine but requires ten minutes cooking. Peas, etc. may also be used.

Clam Broth.—Chop up a dozen little neck clams, put them into a chafing dish with a pint and a half of clam broth or hot water, a walnut of butter, a dash of cayenne, and a single clove. Simmer f··e minutes and serve with toasted bread dice. Some like the broth thickened with a little cracker dust.

Clams Epicurean.—Put into the chafing dish a tea-spoonful of butter, a dash of cayenne, and a dozen small clams; simmer five minutes, add a table-spoonful of sherry, a tea-spoonful of Epicurean sauce and serve on toasted crackers.

Mussels.—Boil two dozen mussels in their shells twenty minutes : when cool remove them from the shells and put them in the chafing dish with a scant table-spoonful of butter, a pinch of curry powder, a gill of claret and a little salt. Dissolve half a tea-spoonful of browned flour in a gill of water, stir into the dish, simmer until the sauce thickens and serve.

Mussels No. 2.—Boil the mussels as in the foregoing recipe. Put into the chafing dish a table-spoonful of butter, when hot add a minced onion and fry it brown. Add a pint of dark beef gravy or hot water thickened with browned flour and colored with kitchen bouquet or kitchen caramel; stir into the sauce a tea-spoonful of paprika, add two dozen boiled Mussels: when thoroughly warmed through, serve.

Mussels No. 3.—Proceed as in the foregoing recipe except that after the onion is cooked add a tea-spoonful of curry powder instead of paprika.

Mussels No. 4.—Put into the chafing dish two table-spoonfuls of table butter, stir it rapidly as it melts and add two heaping table-spoonfuls of pompodoro or tomato paste; mix together thoroughly, add a pint of hot water or better still beef broth, salt and cayenne to taste; in this sauce warm up two dozen mussels.

Steamed Soft Clams.—Wash a dozen soft or paper shell clams thoroughly so as to free them from all sand and grit; put into a chafing dish a scant table-spoonful of butter, put in the clams, shells and all, pile them up in the dish evenly, cover well; light the chafing dish lamp and let them cook in their own juice at least fifteen minutes.

Have ready a hot vegetable dish half filled with hot melted butter, remove the shells and the black skin covering the necks, take hold of the latter, dip the body of each clam into the hot butter and eat them while hot with a slice of Boston brown bread. Oysters and Little Neck Clams may be thus treated.

Soft Clams No. 2.—Remove the shells from a dozen soft or paper shell clams, trim off two-thirds of the tough neck. Cut three thin slices of bacon about four inches long, into dice; put these into the chafing dish and fry them crisp. Add the soft clams and cook them well done in the bacon fat.

Scallops.—Scald two dozen scallops, drain and dry them in a napkin, then fry them in the chafing dish with three table-spoonfuls of butter.

Scallop Stew.—Boil two dozen large scallops thirty minutes in water seasoned with salt, three whole cloves and a bit of mace. Take four table-spoonfuls of table butter, divide it into balls, dredge these with flour; put one-third of the number into the chafing dish and whisk them rapidly, add a gill of the scallop water and as it thickens add one at a time the remainder of the butter balls; when it becomes too thick add a little more of the scallop water using a pint of it altogether. When the ingredients are all used, add salt and cayenne to taste; warm up the scallops in this and just before serving squeeze over the dish the juice of half a lemon.

Scallop Stew.—Parboil the scallops fifteen minutes, put them in the chafing dish with nearly a pint of boiled milk, salt, pepper and a walnut of butter; simmer ten minutes.

Curry of Scallops.—Make a curry sauce by putting into the chafing dish the heaping table-spoonful of olive oil, butter or beef drippings; in this fry a minced onion brown, add a tea-spoonful of curry powder, let it cook a moment and add a pint of consomme or veal broth with salt to taste. Thicken this slightly with a little flour dissolved in cold water, simmer till smooth, add a tea-spoonful of chutney if convenient, and in this sauce warm up a pint of boiled scallops.

Curry of Shrimp.—Put into a chafing dish a table-spoonful of olive oil or butter, a tea-spoonful of chopped onion and fry a delicate brown ; add a tea-spoonful of curry powder. Allow the powder to cook a moment, then add a pint of beef broth ; simmer ten minutes, and add a tea-spoonful of rice flour dissolved in cold water. Let boil until it thickens slightly, then strain into another dish. Open a can of shrimps, rinse them off with cold water, add them to the curry sauce, warm up the dish, then pour over it three tablespoonfuls of fresh orange juice, and serve with boiled rice.

Shrimp Curry No. 2.—Fry a minced onion with a table-spoonful of beef drippings ; when brown add a heaping table-spoonful of curry powder, a tea-spoonful of rice flour, and a heaping saltspoonful of salt ; stir to prevent burning and when the ingredients are in danger of burning add a pint of hot water or broth. Cook until the sauce thickens slightly, strain and add a square of sugar, a heaping table-spoonful of either chutney, apple or cranberry sauce. Put into the sauce a can of shrimps, let the whole warm through thoroughly. Arrange on a platter a border of boiled rice, put the curried shrimp in the centre, squeeze over the shrimp the juice of a lime and over the rice sprinkle the juice of an orange.

Curry of Clams.—Both the little neck and the paper shell clams are very good served as a chafing dish curry, the body part of the soft clam should only be used, as the remainder is somewhat tough. The Little Necks, if cooked too much will be tough. Serve them with a plain curry sauce, made as the sauce for curry of scallops.

Fish Curries.—Cold fish of any kind may be advantageously served in the chafing dish the next day in the form of a curry. All that is necessary is to warm up the fish in the sauce ; care must be exercised however not to break or separate the fish into too fine pieces. Canned salmon, etc., are all excellent and quite convenient for chafing dish cookery either plain or as a curry.

Brook Trout.—Small brook trout may be

sautéed in a chafing dish at table or they may be steamed by filling a hot water dish with hot water, then placing over it a sieve or steamer. The rising steam will cook the fish in a very few minutes. A little butter may be melted in a flat dish used as a cover.

Shad Roe a la Charles W. Brooke.—Scald a pair of shad roe, when cool remove the thin membrane. Put the roe into a small saucepan, cover with white wine, season with half a tea-spoonful of salt, one clove, and a very small piece of mace. Cover the dish and simmer half an hour.

Wash a pint of scallops in cold water, drain, put them into a saucepan and cover with hot water; season with ¼ of a tea-spoonful of salt, an eighth of a bay leaf, four whole allspice and two cloves. Cover the dish and boil half an hour.

Put into a small saucepan a heaping table-spoonful of butter; as it melts whisk it and add a heaping table-spoonful of flour, and a gill of the water in which the scallops were boiled. Whisk rapidly and add another large spoonful of butter, another gill of the scallop water, a tea-spoonful of garlic juice, and ¼ of a tea-spoonful of salt. Stir rapidly until quite smooth and of a velvety appearance, and incorporate in it another spoonful of butter, using three in all.

Allow the sauce to cool a little, then whisk into it the beaten yolks of three eggs.

Drain off the water from the shad roe and the scallops.

Put the roe into a chafing dish, arrange the scallops over them neatly. Now cover the scallops with a thin layer of freshly grated horse-radish, using half a pint. Over this pour the sauce. Light the burner and when the horse-radish is thoroughly heated, serve.

Hamburg Herring.—We are indebted to a distinguished German gourmet for a most toothsome Lenten dainty. It is a fat herring which was put into a smoke house almost alive. When thoroughly smoked it is packed in tins while warm, and sealed. No salt is used in the curing of the dainty; they must therefore be used shortly after the tin is opened.

They taste like fresh herring—one of the sweetest of fish—with the addition of that peculiar appetizing flavor so characteristic of the products of the smoke house.

As a relish they are superior in flavor to kippered or any other style or kind of prepared fish. They are imported from Hamburg, Germany.

Like nearly every other kind of cured fish, this new tidbit requires but warming through to be fully appreciated.

Remove the skin carefully without breaking the flesh, warm it up with a little butter in a chafing dish.

Crab Cakes.—The meat from the hard shell crabs, after boiling, may be made into little cakes, held together with the yolk of an egg, seasoned with salt and pepper, then cooked on both sides in the chafing dish with a small amount of butter or oil.

Curry of Crabs.—Open a can of canned crab meat and turn it out into a dish; examine it for small pieces of shell; in their hurry the canners are sometimes careless and throw in pieces of shell with the meat. Make a curry sauce as for curry of scallops (which see), warm the crab meat in it and serve with boiled rice. The meat from fresh caught crabs of course is to be preferred, but the former is more convenient for city folks.

Soft Shell Crabs.—Clean the crabs by removing the sand pouch, and feathery gill like particles found under the side points of the shell; dry them in a towel, dredge with flour and cook them in a chafing dish until a delicate brown.

Soft Shell Crabs Deviled.—Make a paste of a table-spoonful of curry powder, a tea-spoonful of made English mustard, a tea-spoonful of Epicurean sauce, half a tea-spoonful of salt and a liberal tea-spoonful of oil; spread this paste over the soft crabs and cook them in the chafing dish at table with a liberal quantity of butter or beef drippings. Do not put them into the chafing dish until the fat is very hot.

Lobster Deviled.—Split the tail part of a boiled lobster in two, remove the thread like intestine found in the centre, cover with the paste recommended for Soft Crabs Deviled and cook ten minutes in the chafing dish. The raw lobster is much better for this purpose, but it must be cooked well.

Lobster Pompodoro.—Cut into neat pieces the tail part of two lobsters. Procure from an Italian grocer a can of pompodoro, which is a kind of imported tomato paste. Put into the chafing dish two heaping table-spoonfuls of table butter and three of the paste, whisk rapidly together as they melt, then add a pint of broth or water, simmer until it thickens; warm up the lobster in this. A hundred other food items may be similarly treated.

Lobster Patties.—The small patty shells

may be obtained from the nearest caterer or baker. Warm them before using.

Put into the hot water dish of the chafing dish two thirds of a pint of hot water; over this put the handled dish and in it boil a pint of milk. Dissolve a table-spoonful of flour in a little cold milk, add it to the hot milk; when thick stir in gradually two heaping table-spoonfuls of table butter. Let it become quite thick by cooking. Cut into small pieces the tail part of two boiled lobsters, season well with salt and pepper and over it squeeze a little lemon juice; add the lobster to the sauce, reduce the heat and serve by filling the heated shells with the mixture.

Lobster Cutlets.—Use live lobsters for this purpose. See to it that they are lively, then kill them by cleaving the heads in two; remove the tail part, cut each tail in two and cook the meat thoroughly with beef dripping or butter; season with salt and cayenne.

Lobster Paprika.—Fry in the chafing dish minced onion brown, with a table-spoonful of beef dripping or olive oil, add a pint of good strong beef broth or consomme, a tea-spoonful of the Hungarian mild red pepper called Paprika. Dissolve a tea-spoonful of flour in a gill of cold water, add it also with half a tea-spoonful of salt, simmer until the sauce thickens a little, then add boiled lobster meat cut up, or in cutlet form ; simmer five minutes longer and serve. A tea-spoonful of pompodoro will improve this sauce.

Curry of Lobster.—A delicious curry may be made from lobster as follows :—Put into chafing dish a table-spoonful of butter. When it foams add a heaping table-spoonful of minced onion. Let the onion brown well, then add a heaping tea-spoonful of curry powder. Allow this to cook from three to five minutes or until it becomes almost black. Add a pint of rice water, or soup stock if preferred; season with half a tea-spoonful of salt, simmer five minutes and add a pint more of the rice water ; simmer until reduced nearly one-half, then warm up the lobster in the sauce and serve with boiled rice. There must be sufficient sauce to allow the meat to almost float about in it. The rice water referred to is water in which rice was boiled. It is scientifically of more nutritive value than the rice itself.

Rice for Curry.—The essential point to be gained is that after boiling, each grain of rice must be distinct and unbroken, yet tender and to every appearance fairly ready to burst yet remains intact. To accomplish this a small quantity of rice must be cooked in a large volume of water. An ordinary half pint cupful of rice should be boiled in at least a gallon of water. It will surprise the uninitiated when they compare the bulk of the rice before and after cooking. The rice should be first well washed in several waters; reject all husks and imperfect grains; put the rice into cold water slightly salted and boil about twenty-five minutes. Old rice requires a little longer cooking. The grains should occasionally be tested, and when a slight pressure will crush them they are done. If boiled until the grains burst the rice is spoiled for serving with curry. If boiled in a small volume of water the rice is also rendered useless as the grains will stick together. After boiling, the rice should be placed over the range where it will throw off the moisture absorbed in the boiling.

Lobster a la Newburg.—Lobster a la Newburg is now a popular dish on our restaurant bills of fare.

A recent writer on gastronomic matters, in speaking of the origin of the dish said: "It was invented by a resident of Newburg on the Hudson, who named it after his native town."

Were it not for the fact that a number of

the old habitues of Delmonico's are still alive to prove the falsity of this statement, the future epicurean historian might be led to make the same error as past writers have made in their attempt to trace the origin of many of the popular dishes of to-day.

Lobster a la Newburg was invented by Ben Wenberg. "Ben" as he was called was in every sense of the word a true gastronome. Mr. Wenberg probably did more to popularize the chafing dish than any one of the patrons of Delmonico's. In those good old days Wenberg would gather about him a half a dozen congenial spirits, and cook for them at table the stewed lobster which honestly deserves to be named after him. Old Charles Delmonico once put a la Wenberg on the bill of fare in honor of its inventor but the modesty of the epicure objected so earnestly that to please him the first half of the name was reversed and the dish became Newburg instead of Wenberg. It is made as follows:

Put into a chafing dish three ounces of butter, stir it as it creams; add a gill of water containing a teaspoonful of flour, season with salt and cayenne; pour in a pint of boiled milk, stir and simmer till smooth. Beat up the yolks of three raw eggs, let the boiled milk, etc. cool a little by reducing the heat, then add the egg, half a gill of sherry ; work all together and in it warm up the meat from the boiled lobsters.

Almost every cook has a different way of making sauce ; the most popular one is the cream sauce usually served with Terrapin. A friend of Mr. Wenberg's told me he did not use eggs in his.

Here is another formula.

La Newburg.—Divide two medium sized lobsters in halves. Remove the coral and creamy green fat and put one side. Put into a chafing dish two ounces of table butter. When it creams whisk into it a gill of Madeira or sherry. Simmer until reduced one-half. Beat together the yolks of three eggs and half a pint of rich cream, season with a little salt and cayenne pepper. Divide three ounces of table butter into little balls, dredge these with flour and one by one add to the sauce, whisking thoroughly as each butter ball is added. Reduce to a paste the coral and the tom-alley and stir into the sauce. Simmer until the sauce becomes of a creamy consistency, then add the lobster, mix and serve.

Shrimp Patties.—This is a delicious luncheon dish and may be prepared at table by the lady, as the pattie shells may be obtained from the nearest caterer or baker. Put into the chafing dish a pint of hot milk, add to it a table-spoonful of flour previously dissolved in a little cold milk, simmer until thick and stir into it gradually two ounces of butter and half a tea-spoonful of salt. Open a can of New Orleans shrimp, take them out of the can and the linen bag in which they come and rinse in cold water; cut them in two and send to table with heated patty shells; warm up the shrimp in the sauce in the chafing dish, fill the patty shells and serve.

Shrimps in Butter.—Put into the chafing dish two table-spoonfuls of butter, toss the shrimp about in it, add the juice of half a lime, a dash of cayenne, a gill of water; cook three minutes and serve.

Codfish Tongues.—Scald the codfish tongues a moment, drain and cut them each into four pieces, cook them six minutes in the chafing dish with two table-spoonfuls of butter, add the juice of half a lemon, a sprig of parsley chopped up and a tea-spoonful of mushroom catsup.

Codfish Tongues No. 2.—Boil three codfish tongues in water slightly salted thirty minutes and send them to table for the chafing dish.

Put into the hot water dish half a pint of hot
water, over this place the chafing dish proper.
Bruise a clove of garlic, put it in the upper
dish with a heaping table-spoonful of butter,
whisk it with a wooden spoon, add a table-
spoonful of flour and a pint of milk ; stir con-
stantly and whisk into it the beaten yolks of
two eggs ; season with salt and pepper, warm
up the codfish tongues in the sauce, before
serving, add the juice of a lemon.   Care must
be exercised not to allow the eggs to curdle.

Frogs Legs.—Boil four pairs of frogs legs in
milk forty minutes and send to table for the
chafing dish.   They may afterwards be prepared for the guests by warming them up in
any one of the sauces heretofore recommended.

Frog Leg Patties.—Boil the legs until the
meat falls from the bone ; remove the bones
and send the meat to table with small patty
shells previously warmed.   Prepare a sauce as
for lobster patties, warm the meat up in it and
serve.

Curry of Salmon.—Cold boiled salmon
may be served as a curry in a chafing dish
and a salmon steak cooked in a curry sauce is
very good eating, but there is no better way
of serving canned salmon than as a curry.
The only point is to be sure to buy the best

known brand of canned salmon. Fry a minced onion brown in the chafing dish with an overflowing table-spoonful of olive oil, add two tea-spoonfuls of curry powder, let cook a moment and add a pint of hot water, a table-spoonful of flour dissolved in cold water, a table-spoonful of tomato catsup or chutney, and a little salt, stir, simmer until the sauce thickens, then add the contents of a one pound can of salmon to the sauce; let it warm through before serving.

Eels.—Cut into three inch pieces two medium sized eels and parboil them half an hour; dry in a napkin. Cut into dice two medium sized slices of fat salt pork, fry the pork out and in the fat finish cooking the eels; add a little lemon juice before serving.

Stewed Eels.—Boil two pounds of medium sized salt water eels half an hour and send to table for the chafing dish. Put into the chafing dish two scant tea-spoonfuls of butter, a minced onion, a bit of mace and half a tea-spoonful of salt. Allow the onion to cook until it is in danger of becoming from straw to a darker color, then add a pint of boiled milk; add a scant tea-spoonful of flour dissolved in a little cold milk, when smooth add the eels, simmer five minutes longer before serving.

Curried Eels.—Put into a chafing dish two table-spoonfuls of olive oil, before it gets too hot add a tea-spoonful of curry powder, now add a few pieces of cold eels, stir them round or shake the dish, to cover the pieces evenly with the curry; when thoroughly heated through, serve.

Curry of Eels.—Put into a chafing dish a heaping table-spoonful of butter, a minced onion, a tea-spoonful of curry powder, six pieces of raw eel, each about an inch long, cover and shake the dish to prevent burning; cook five minutes and add a pint of veal broth, or better still, fish consommé, a tea-spoonful of chutney or tomato sauce. Serve with boiled rice.

Turtle Steak.—Florida sends us turtle steak in cans, it is very convenient at times to have a can of it in the house; in fact, all modern canned goods are quite useful and convenient in chafing dish cookery. The prejudice against such prepared food is absurd. Cook the steak in butter, season with salt, cayenne, a few spoonfuls of good sherry or port, and serve on toast.

Turtle Steak Deviled.—Add to half a gill

of orange juice a tea-spoonful of corn powder and salt-spoonful of mustard, spread it over a turtle steak and cook the steak in a chafing dish five minutes on each side.

Turtle Steak a la Henry Guy Carleton.— Melt two ounces of butter in a chafing dish, add a table-spoonful of mushroom catsup, two table-spoonfuls of currant jelly, a gill of port wine, a dash of cayenne and a little salt. In this simmer the steak till tender; finally add the juice of half a lime and serve.

Curry of Prawns.—Put into a chafing dish a heaping table-spoonful of butter, when hot add a chopped spring onion or a young leek, cook a few moments and add a heaping tea-spoonful of curry powder, stir to prevent burning, allow it to cook a moment and add half a pint of hot water or beef stock, one small sour apple peeled and cut into dice, a square of sugar and a tea-spoonful of epicurean sauce; cover and simmer until the apple is cooked, then add another half pint of beef broth, a quart of boiled prawns add to the sauce, heat them through, season with a small quantity of salt and a table-spoonful of tomato catsup, pour out the curry on to a hot platter, surround it with a border of boiled rice, squeeze over the curry the juice of half a lemon and serve.

Terrapin.—Prepared terrapin is always to be had in New York and for this reason it is often seen served out of season. Thus prepared it simply requires warming up in the chafing dish, with a little sherry added.

Terrapin No. 2.—A great deal of care should be exercised in selecting the live terrapin. This is the first and at the same time the most important step in the preparation of the dish. The best should be fresh caught and fresh and healthy looking, a pen terrapin spends most of its time seeking freedom. It worries under restraint and will prove poor eating, the liver will taste so rank that one can hardly eat it. The legs of the penned terrapin will show ebrasions on the under side where the poor thing injured itself seeking an avenue of escape.

The right kind selected, plunge it into boiling water and boil fifteen minutes; when cool remove the under shell, the skin from the legs, the gall bag and entrails and throw this refuse away. Put the remainder into a saucepan, season it with salt and a dash of cayenne; add just water enough to prevent burning and simmer an hour. Now add a gill of good sherry and put it away as it is better the next day. Put into the chafing dish a scant table-spoonful of table butter, and a salt-spoonful of flour, rub this smooth and add the terrapin with two table-spoonfuls of sherry, cook three minutes and serve.

Snails.—Rinse a quart of snails in cold water slightly salted, drain and boil them half an hour in barely sufficient water to cover them; when cool pick them out of the shells, cut off the nose and the tip end of the tails, put them back in the shells, then put them into the chafing dish, add half a pint of strong beef gravy or broth, a table-spoonful each of epicurean sauce and claret, salt to taste, simmer until the sauce is nearly evaporated.

Snails on Toast.—Boil the snails as in the foregoing recipe, pick them out of the shells and chop them fine, season slightly with salt, white pepper and nutmeg, warm this hash in the chafing dish with a little butter, when ready serve on thin buttered toast.

Poached Eggs.—In parts of New England they call this dish "poached eggs." Beat up six eggs, add a salt-spoonful of salt and a pint of milk. Put over the hot water dish the chafing dish proper; put into the latter a table-spoonful of butter, when melted stir in the egg mixture and keep stirring it with a fork until it sets. Serve on toast.

Poached Eggs.—Put into the hot water dish of the chafing dish, six poached egg rings, surround them with hot water, carefully break an egg into each ring and when firm place on buttered toast.

Eggs with Cheese.—Break into a well buttered chafing dish six eggs, stir them back and forth with a fork as for scrambled eggs; when set, sprinkle a few drops of vinegar over the eggs, salt and pepper to taste and finally a liberal layer of grated cheese.

Eggs with Asparagus Tops.—Proceed as in the foregoing recipe except to omit the cheese and substitute asparagus points from the asparagus left from the preceding dinner. When the asparagus points are hot, serve.

Eggs with Brown Butter.—Allow three heaping table-spoonfuls of butter to cook in the chafing dish until almost black. Drop into it carefully four eggs and as they cook, throw the butter over them with a spoon. When well done place on thin toast, add a few drops of tarragon vinegar and serve.

Eggs with Chives.—Break six eggs into the chafing dish proper, which should be placed over the hot water dish, add to them a tea-spoonful of chopped chives, a dash of paprika, a little salt, and serve.

Eggs a la Brisbane.—Mr. Arthur Brisbane, the distinguished journalist, prepares scrambled eggs in a chafing dish and serves with them a rich truffled sauce called sauce Perigord. It is a delightful late supper dish; those who can afford it are referred to Mr. Murrey's more pretentious works for the recipe of the sauce.

Boiled Eggs.—The chafing dish is just the thing for boiling eggs at table in hot weather.

Eggs with Curry.—Sprinkle over six scrambled eggs while they are cooking half a teaspoonful of dry curry powder and serve on toast.

Eggs with Garlic Oil.—Divide a bulb of garlic into cloves, remove the outside husks, cut each clove into thin strips lengthwise, put them into half a pint bottle and fill the bottle with olive oil; in a week the oil will take on the flavor of the garlic and use this oil for frying eggs. While cooking keep the cover on as the oil spatters.

Eggs with Kidneys.—Scald three mutton kidneys, remove the thin skin over them and cut them into thin slices. Put into the chafing dish a table-spoonful of beef drippings, when hot add a chopped Bermuda onion; when slightly browned add the kidneys, salt and white pepper to taste, cook the kidneys three minutes, add four raw eggs and when the latter becomes firm, serve.

Kidneys with Bacon.—Put into the chafing dish two table-spoonfuls of chopped bacon. When well cooked add three scalded, skinned and sliced kidneys, cook four minutes, season with a little white pepper, and serve.

Kidneys and Potatoes.—Wash, peel and cut into small dice two medium sized raw potatoes. Scald and skin three mutton kidneys, quarter them, chop up sufficient celery to make a tea-spoonful. Put into a chafing dish a scant table-spoonful of butter; when quite hot, put in the potatoes, stir to prevent sticking to the dish, add the celery, then the kidneys and half a pint of good rich brown gravy. Season with salt and pepper and a table-spoonful of mushroom catsup. Cover and simmer six minutes and serve.

Kidneys with Mushrooms.—Scald, skin and quarter six lambs' kidneys, cut into thin slices the contents of half a can of French mushrooms. Put into the chafing dish a heaping table-spoonful of butter, a minced onion and a very small piece of a bay leaf; when the onion is quite brown add a tea-spoonful of browned flour; stir into the dish a pint of beef broth and a scant tea-spoonful of kitchen bouquet; season with half a tea-spoonful of salt and a salt-spoonful of white pepper, add the kidneys and the mushrooms, stir to prevent burning and cook six minutes.

Curried Veal Chops.—Mix together a heaping table-spoonful of curry powder, two salt-spoonfuls of salt, a tea-spoonful of " made " mustard, a dash of cayenne, a tea-spoonful of epicurean sauce, and olive oil enough to make a paste ; spread a little of this on both sides of the chops, then dip in beaten egg, roll in bread crumbs and fry in the chafing dish.

Veal Tomato Sauce.—Cut into neat slices a small quantity of cold roast veal. Put into the chafing dish two table-spoonfuls of butter, three table-spoonfuls of pompodoro—Italian tomato paste—and a pint of veal broth, salt and cayenne to taste. When smooth add the meat and serve when quite hot.

Curry of Sweetbreads.—Select two fine sweetbreads, scald them and remove from them all sinews, etc. Put them into water slightly salted, cover and parboil half an hour; drain, and keep in cold water till wanted. Prepare a plain curry sauce in the chafing dish ; slice the sweetbreads, cook them in the sauce ten minutes and serve.

Calf's Liver with Bacon.—Cut three small thin slices of bacon into inch pieces and cook them well done in a chafing dish, add to the dish one and one half more calf's liver sliced quite thin. Cook until the liver begins to curl up on the sides.

Calf's Liver with Gravy.—Prepare in the chafing dish a brown gravy, similar to, (instructions for Kidneys with Mushrooms) and in this sauce simmer three thin slices of calf's liver.

Roast Beef for Breakfast or Luncheon.—Put into the chafing dish a table-spoonful of beef drippings ; when hot, add a medium sized red onion, chopped fine, two whole cloves, four pepper corns, broken, two allspice, the smallest bit of bay leaf, a sprig each of green parsley and celery. When the onion is quite brown, add a pint and a half of hot water, or better still beef broth. Simmer six minutes, add salt and cayenne. Dissolve a heaping table-spoonful of flour in a gill of cold water ; rub it smooth, add a few spoonfuls of the hot sauce to the flour, then pour it into the dish, stir well and add half a tea-spoonful of kitchen boquet ; in this warm up cold roast beef.

Steak Rechauffe.—Divide into small balls

four ounces of butter, dredge these with flour. Put one fourth of them into a chafing dish and over the hot water dish ; as it melts whisk it rapidly and add a pint of hot water, whisk rapidly and gradually add one fourth more of the butter balls, repeat this process until the butter is all used. Let the sauce cool a little, season with sauce and white pepper. Bruise all over a piece of cold broiled sirloin steak the juice of three cloves of garlic ; now return to the sauce, and add to it while off the flame, the yolks of two raw eggs, if too hot the eggs will separate ; in this sauce warm up the steak.

Tripe.—Select the double tripe if possible ; boil a pound of it an hour and a half. When wanted warm it up in a sauce made as per recipe for cold steak.

Curried Tripe.—Rinse off a pound of fresh tripe in scalding hot water, drain it, cut it into conveniently sized pieces, and boil them in water slightly salted, an hour and a half, then add the tripe to a plain curry sauce made in the chafing dish and serve with boiled rice.

Curried Tripe and Onions.—Cut into slices three Bermuda or white onions. Fry in the chafing dish a delicate brown, with three table-spoonfuls of olive oil ; strew over the onion a tea-spoonful of curry-powder, add half a pound of cold boiled tripe, cover the dish, and shake the pan to prevent burning; when the onion is cooked, serve.

Chops and Cutlets.—It is really surprising how quickly and how very perfect chops, steaks and cutlets of all kinds can be cooked in a chafing dish at table. The dish must invariably be kept covered to prevent the hot fat from jumping out. I have cooked chops perfectly in from four to seven minutes, the variation in time depending upon the thickness of the meat.

Pig's Feet.—It is more convenient and more economical to buy pig's feet already boiled, split them in two and saute in the chafing dish. Care must be exercised to use sufficient fat to prevent sticking to the dish.

Potatoes Lyonnaise.—Cut two red onions into quarters, then into strips and fry them in a chafing dish with either butter or beef drippings. Cut up into small slices five medium sized new potatoes—boiled—and cook them well with the onion.

Potatoes a l'Ete.—Peel and slice two raw new potatoes. Put into the chafing dish a heaping table-spoonful of beef dripping. When quite hot lay in the slices of potato; when a delicate brown on one side turn each piece.

Potato Dice.—Cut raw potatoes into dice and cook them well in the chafing dish. Time for three potatoes ten minutes, stir to prevent burning.

Mushrooms.—Remove all grit and peel a dozen freshly gathered mushrooms, remove the stems; melt a tea-spoonful of butter in the chafing dish and before it gets too hot lift the dish off and put it on a plate. Cover the bottom of the dish with mushrooms; on top of each mushroom put a bit of butter the size of a marble; season each with a little salt and pepper. Return the dish to the flame, and cook three minutes.

Puff-balls.—At certain seasons puff-balls are found in profusion in the fields and pastures. What surprises me is that so few people know that they are a most delightful, nutritious and wholesome fungi. They should be gathered when the inside is of a creamy white; when touched with a streak of yellow, or are spongy they are too old. Peel them, cut them into thin slices and fry them in the chafing dish plain. They may be also stewed in the chafing dish.

Green Peas.—When green peas become dry and old they require considerable cooking but when fresh and a beautiful green they require but little cooking and this little is best accomplished in a chafing dish. After removing them from the pods, put them in the chafing dish. To a quart of peas add water enough to cover the bottom of the pan, say a little less than a pint; the steam arising from the water cooks the peas and the heat from the alcohol flame is so intense that the peas are cooked so quickly they retain their delicate green color. Season with salt, white pepper, and be liberal with the best butter.

Canned Peas.—Open the can, rinse off the peas with cold water, then simply warm them in the chafing dish; longer cooking spoils them.

Chicken Gallosch.—Cut into dice two medium sized raw potatoes. Put into the chafing dish a table-spoonful of olive oil; when hot add the potato, stir to prevent burning, and after five minutes cooking add, half a teaspoonful of paprika, half a pint of hot water, a clove of garlic, half a pound of cold roast chicken cut into dice, half a salt-spoonful of salt; stir occasionally, cover while cooking and when the potatoes are done serve.

Beef Gallosch.—Proceed as in the foregoing recipe, using half an onion instead of the clove of garlic, and flank steak cut small instead of chicken; but it should be raw meat.

Pork Tenderloin.—Fry an onion slightly in the chafing dish, with a table-spoonful of butter; cut into dice a small pork tenderloin, add it to the dish and cook it thoroughly; now add half a pint of gravy or broth, salt and cayenne to taste and two warm, boiled new potatoes cut into dice, cover and serve with a cucumber salad for breakfast or luncheon.

The Mysteries of Welsh Rabbits.—Everybody who has tasted a rightly composed Welsh rabbit likes it, but not every one dares to repeat the indulgence because of the difficulty some people have of digesting it.

I have discovered a simple method of making the dish digestible, and first made my discovery known through the culinary column of the New York *Herald*.

The secret is to add paprika to the cheese.

It may surprise the lover of Welsh rabbits to learn that by the addition of this simple condiment its indigestibility is overcome.

The formula for making the digestible Welsh rabbit is as follows :—

For a party of four grate a pound of what is known as " full cream American cheese ; " put into the chafing dish a " walnut " of butter ; as it melts stir it with a wooden spoon to grease the bottom of the dish, then add the grated cheese. As the cheese melts, stir it, and add a table-spoonful of old American or imported ale. It will now begin to stick to the dish ; to prevent this, stir and gradually add spoonfuls of ale until the mixture is smooth and velvety in appearance. Stir into the cheese a table-spoonful of paprika ; mix well, and when of a creamy consistency put spoonfuls of it on hot, dry toast.

Hot plates are absolutely necessary.

The amount of ale required varies according to the quality of the cheese, but about one and a half gills of ale is all that is required ; should this amount thin out the cheese too much, the mixture must be rapidly stirred to evaporate the unnecessary moisture.

CHAFING DISHES

The Chafing Dishes made by the Gorham Mfg. Co. are of superior quality. They are constructed of hard metal, silver soldered at every joint, perfectly finished, and very heavily silver plated. A variety of styles and sizes are made, with various pieces, to be used separately, or combined.

GORHAM MFG CO., SILVERSMITHS,

BROADWAY AND 19TH ST., NEW

YORK. MAKERS OF SOLID SILVER

WARES AND THE CELEBRATED

GORHAM PLATE.